Lines for Everyday Living

Lines for

AN ESSANDESS SPECIA

Everyday Living

by Chet Long

DITION 📖 NEW YORK

Lines for Everyday Living

SBN 671–10508–6

To Jodi

Lines for Everyday Living

Give a Friend a Book

Give a friend a book to read;
You'll be giving of yourself.
You'll become a part of
That book that joins his shelf.
Every time he pulls it down
          to read a line or two,
He'll think of where it came from
          and his thoughts will dwell on you.
Give a friend a book to read,
But choose the book with care.
Know that when he looks at it,
You'll be standing there.
Other gifts may come and go,
But books become a bond.
They mellow with the passing time
          and capture the beyond.
Books, like lasting friendships,
          Should be chosen carefully.
Think: I am a part of this;
          And a part of this is me.

God, let me have a goal to seek
    And never let me make it.
Please, keep it just beyond my reach,
    And don't let me forsake it.
God, give me something up ahead
    To which I can aspire;
And keep my aim and interest high
    So that I will never tire.

*　　*　　*

Let me seek until I die,
    Be ever stepping up;
Let me drink life to the full,
    But never drain the cup.

Any kindness you convey
    Returns in kind another day.

Trouble will knock, you may be sure,
You have to expect it some day.
But when trouble knocks and you knock back,
It quickly hurries away.

If friendships in life is what you are seeking,
Check what you're saying before you start
            speaking.

Do a job when it has to be done,
And get it out of the way.
Don't put it off 'til tomorrow;
That's Yesterday's name for Today.

Here's a thought to remember
When you feel that the going is rough,
If you've learned to mind your own business
In a crisis, you've learned enough.

Concerned about life's challenges?
These words may help a bit:
The competition's as scared of you
As you're afraid of it.

If you desire to improve yourself,
Remember this one fact:
Act the way you'd like to be,
Then you'll be the way you act.

A Lesson on Life

Priscilla Penelope Poppins
Was a proper person, I'm told.
She attended her church every Sunday
And her virtues she loudly extolled.
It's true that by Tuesday, religion
Was lost for the rest of the week;
But Saturday found her repentant,
And on Sunday in church, she was meek.
She lived by the rule of so many:
God rated one day in seven.
And she believed that her one hour in church
Insured her passport to Heaven.

Priscilla Penelope Poppins
Had a bitter lesson to learn,
That the passport to Heaven's not handed to us
It's something each person must earn.
Don't be like the proper Miss Poppins
Think of God not one day, but seven.
It will add to the joys you'll receive in this life
And you won't have to worry 'bout Heaven.

Don't waste today on yesterday;
With dusk each day must stop.
And hashing over what might have been
Is like watering last year's crop.

Take your problems as they come;
No point to frown or fret.
Hurryin' brings worryin',
So why get all upset?

One thing you must note,
If you want to succeed;
To have a fine harvest,
You must first sow the seed.

Friendship, like old china,
Is beautiful and rare.
If it's broken, you can mend it;
But the crack is always there.

What you're trying to do,
Do with all your might.
Things half done
Are never done right.

Grandma had some wise words
That all of us should follow:
"Flattery's like tobacco;
Good to chew, but not to swallow."

Life Is Like a Fountain Pen

Life is like a fountain pen
That's filled to the brim for use.
Some people use it wisely;
Some display abuse.
Once you've used the ink of life,
The pen is dry and dead.
The mark you leave behind will show
The kind of life you led.
Some people write a masterpiece
Before their time is done.
Some waste the contents of the pen
Before their setting sun.
Life is like a fountain pen,
Filled to write your fate.
Get set, and try;
The ink might dry,
And then 'twill be too late.

Never trust beyond recall.
The farther you lean,
The farther you fall.

Here's to the really great men—
The men who have a will—
Who know all things are possible
With diligence and skill.

Live and Learn

We seek, we strive, and we acquire;
    But after victory's won,
We turn our thoughts toward other goals
    Beyond tomorrow's sun.
If only we would stop to think
    Of all we have today,
We'd find the game of life more fun
    In knowing how to play.

The world would be a better place
    And not so filled with dread,
If those who point a finger
    Hold out a hand instead.

The dreams you dream for tomorrow
    Will vanish and fade away,
Unless you know that tomorrow
    Depends on what happens today.

Whatever your task is, do it!
    Do it with all your might!
It's better by far to complete it
    Than to explain why it wasn't done right.

If you are really anxious
        To make your life complete,
Try to find the good that's there
        In everyone you meet.

For the problems in life
You'd like to surmount,
Don't count time,
Make time count.

The time you spend in thinking
Is never, ever, wasted.
It's through the action from your thought
That victory is tasted.

The more looking around you do in life,
      The oftener you'll find
That anger is the fickle wind
      That blows out the lamp of the mind.

Life is a temporary home
      In which there's always movement.
And the largest room in each one's "home"
      Is the room for self-improvement.

One thought we ought to keep with us
      As we're moving along our way;
The harvest we reap in the future
      Is the seed we're sowing today.

Worry's Like a Rocking Chair

Worry's like a rocking chair;
It gives a lot of action.
It can make you awfully dizzy, too,
Removing satisfaction.

Worry is a poison vial
Smashed inside your heart.
It wipes away the brightest smile
And tears your plans apart.

Worry is a worthless check
Paid on a debt not due.
It pays with your life on something
That's destroying the good in you.

Worry's a meaningless habit;
It never gains a thing.
It teaches a colorless, doleful song
That you force yourself to sing.

Yes, worry can surely be likened
To that family rocking chair.
It'll keep you moving constantly,
But'll never get you there.

Whatever your job may be in life
     Here's a spot of good advice:
It's nice to be important,
     But more important to be nice.

Here's a bit of timeless wisdom,
     Good for old or young,
It's better by far to slip with the foot
     Than to slip with a careless tongue.

You can't fool yourself, so do your best;
     And after that is done,
Be glad you tried; be satisfied,
     Whether you've lost or won.

Setting your sights on an obstacle
    Seems to make it bigger.
Most people have a good aim in life,
    But too few pull the trigger.

The secret of real happiness
    Is what's inside of you.
And the most important part of it
    Is liking what you do.

In this busy life with all its strife,
    One axiom's well worth knowing:
It's all right to pray for the harvest,
    But you'd better keep on hoeing.

Smile, Smile, Smile

Of all the things in life worthwhile,
    Few can beat a friendly smile.
It will work in any place or season . . .
    It doesn't need a special reason.
It's usually returned in style;
    Try it. Find out why it pays to smile.

People who talk
        Without checking sources
Are often guilty
        Of faulty discourses.

If you have a dollar, and I have a dollar,
        And we swap, neither has gained.
But with two ideas and a similar trade,
        Each a new thought has attained.

Wisely choose the words you use,
Though they be dull or clever.
Good or bad, gay or sad,
Once used, words stand forever.

How Troubles Multiply

I had a little problem
    Which I just shoved aside.
I didn't try to solve it;
    I thought that it had died.
But that tricky little problem
    Doubled as it grew,
And then it doubled once again,
    Then multiplied by two.
It wasn't much to start with—
    Hardly worth its name.
But that nasty little problem
    Must carry all the blame.
If I had just respected it
    And solved it at the start,
It never would have grown so big,
    And torn my plans apart.

It never pays to speak in haste
    When temper holds its sway.
Because the words you're bound to speak
    Will bring regrets that stay.

Those who hesitate to start
    Toward goals that might be won
Are passed by others with far less
    Who started and got it done.

A thing you should remember
    That will serve you in the end:
Naught's gained by winning an argument
    That loses you a friend.

Learning is an accomplishment in which you
can take pride;
But knowledge isn't worth its salt unless it is
applied.

Here's a tried and true formula that's good
every day:
Say what you mean and mean what you say!

He who first thinks something through
Knows exactly what to do.

Stop and Think

We take so much for granted
    As we travel on our way.
We get comfortably accustomed
    To the joys of every day.
Too often as we hurry on
    Toward some unknown tomorrow,
We fail to comprehend what's ours
    Is only ours to borrow.

A good rule to follow
    And live to the letter:
Don't criticize another's work,
    Unless you can do it better.

Before you complain about your lot,
    Take time to look around.
Folks who are doing more with less
    Are everywhere to be found.

No wiser words have ever come
From philosophic lips:
"Responsibility on the shoulder
Leaves no room for chips."

If you want to, spend time viewing it;
But no task is done without doing it.

Here's an old motto, yet up-to-date:
Never envy—emulate!

Peace of Mind

Peace of mind is found inside
    You, not in your surrounding.
You find it in the way you live,
    In the life you are expounding.
Some folks make a lifetime quest
    In vain to find this peace.
But they seek it in such far-off spots
    Their search can never cease.
They seek it in the great outdoors,
    Among the crowded throng,
They look for it and grope for it
    And hope a whole life long.
Don't try to find peace somewhere else;
    Your search will ne'er be done.
Look inside for peace of mind;
    It's there for everyone.

The future belongs to those who say,
"I will do my best today."

As you pass through life, never forget
Strangers are friends you've never met.

If you want to find a man's true worth,
Look for the good he has done on earth.

A smile is worth its weight in gold.
It can't be bought, it can't be sold.
But give a smile, and when you do,
It always comes right back to you.

Every time you smile away
　　　A teardrop on a rainy day,
You bring to life your inner pride,
　　　And come out on the sunny side.

Smiles can heal when someone's ill.
Smiles can talk and smiles can thrill.

Of all the gifts a friend might treasure.
Your smile can give the greatest pleasure.

So smile; and you'll find when you do,
The whole darn world smiles back at you.

To make this world seem more worthwhile,
Be slower to anger and quicker to smile.

Remember this line if your routine is slack:
Stay on your toes, or you'll land on your back.

The result that emerges from life's greatest test:
He profits the most who serves others the best.

Do It Now

If you have a kind thought
    For someone who's dear,
Speak it today
    While that person is near.

If someone is sick
    And you're able to write;
Don't wait 'til tomorrow,
    Write him tonight.

It's too late for sympathy
    After he's gone.
The life here today
    May have faded by dawn.

If you have a kind thought,
    Pursue it this hour.
The dead cannot hear
    Or smell of the flower.

No one knows the future,
    So make this your vow;
If you can spread kindness,
    Don't wait; do it now!

A mode that's never out of style
Is the facial expression we call a smile!

Living is one continuous test;
And the least you can do is to do your best.

Words have wings and fly away,
But the thoughts they leave will always stay.

If you were to count your possessions
    Whatever might be your wealth,
No assets you own would have greater worth
    Than peace of mind and health.

Some cross their fingers, hope for the best
        and plead;
Others work with both hands to meet
        every test and succeed.

If only one word were a rule of life,
"Reciprocity" might well do.
Doing unto others
What you'd like done unto you!

Life Is Like a Baseball Game

Life is like a baseball game;
Before the season's through,
You rotate your position,
And the score is up to you.

You have your turn at bat each day.
You also play defense.
On good days, the game is easy.
On bad days, the game is tense.

You can't escape an error,
That happens along the way.
And errors can be quite costly,
Depending upon the play.

You're bound to strike out a time or two,
Yet, all of us have hits.
But the game is won by the guy who sticks,
Not by the one who quits.

Some of us are major leaguers,
Some can't make that grade.
But bush-league, minors, majors,
All can win; it's how we've played.

Lift your eyes and look around;
You can't see the stars when you gaze at the
ground.

One rule in life it's good to believe in:
You won't get ahead spending time getting
even.

Life is for living; time doesn't wait.
Use it and live it, or you'll vegetate.

Four little words to make dreams come true,
But don't stop to count them—
Dig in, and do.

The climb to the top isn't made in a day.
And many's the obstacle found on the way.
But he who keeps climbing whatever besets,
He who keeps reaching up, usually gets.

In the search for fame and fortune
One thing to understand
Is that no great victory's ever reached
Lest *heart* joins *head* and *hand*.

Our Country

To be able to say what we want to say,
    To worship the way we choose;
To be able to work at the task we select,
    To compete; to win or to lose.
The right to be wrong,
    To be weak or be strong;
The right of a man to his dreams . . .
    From the choice of a wife,
To a whole way of life . . .
    That's what America means.

It's better to do what you think is right
And fail when you try to do it,
Than to think it's right, but never try,
And then have to live to rue it.

Be not inclined toward hasty words;
Think before you start.
There's nothing good in a bitter tongue
That comes from a bitter heart.

If someone says you're average,
Don't be content, then stop.
Remember, average is just as close
To the bottom as to the top.

Set a Good Example

Everything you say in life
And everything you do
Guides another on his way,
The one who follows you.

So watch your actions, take great care
In all you do and say.
No matter what your task may be,
You are marking someone's way.

You're setting an example
For those who think you're great;
You're teaching through the way you live;
You're helping to create.

Great or small, it's true of all,
There's someone watching you.
Consider those who'll follow
In everything you do.

Consider twice 'ere any vice
You let betray this trust.
You're someone's best example,
So do your best. You must!

Here's a little reminder
To note along life's way:
The hardest part of making good
Is doing it every day.

Why not try, for size, a smile;
Forget the thought of tears.
It will not add more years to your life,
But it will add life to your years.

You have to face life's problems
And do the best you can.
You'll never get experience
On an easy-payment plan.

As you go through life
You belatedly find
That each precious day
Is one of a kind.

When you're faced with adversity,
Or in a corner pinned,
Remember, kites fly highest
Against, not with, the wind.

Index of First Lines

61